WHAT IS AIKIDO?

AIKIDO in Daily Life

202 pages with 484 photographs in black-and-white and 4 drawing cuts in text.
Cloth binding with laminated jacket.
L. C. Catalog Card No. 66-23397

WHAT IS AIKIDO?

by
KOICHI TOHEI
*Chief Instructor at
the General Headquarters Arena
of Aikido*

RIKUGEI PUBLISHING HOUSE
TOKYO, JAPAN

First printing: September 1962
Eighth printing: October 1974
Library of Congress Catalog Card No. 62-19252

ISBN–0–87040–146–7

Publishers:
Rikugei Publishing House, Tokyo, Japan

Distributors:
Japan Publications Trading Company
San Francisco · Tokyo

Printed in Japan

FOREWORD

FROM February 1961 to March 1962, I traveled in Hawaii and California where I tried to popularize Aikido. I was happy to learn that my first volume in English on Aikido had attracted a large number of readers among those who were practicing the art as well as many others.

At the same time, many persons asked me, "Would you bring out on your next visit here a handbook to enable us to explain briefly what Aikido is and what its salient features are? We ourselves understand Aikido techniques and principles but we have difficulty in explaining them to others."

This book is the answer to those requests.

The purpose of Aikido lies not in trying to make people strong in the arts of self-defense but in helping them learn the eternal truths that form the basis of Aikido and manifest themselves in Aikido practice. Aikido helps the individual to attain the greatest heights of human personality, cleanse his mental and spiritual environment and help to make the world a brighter place in which to live.

I shall be happy if this book can in some measure help the reader in attaining the objectives of Aikido.

KOICHI TOHEI

TOKYO, JAPAN
July 1962

Prof. Morihei Uyeshiba
Originator of Aikido

Performance of Professor Uyeshiba as he gives lessons.

Kisshomaru Uyeshiba
The Director of the General Headquarters Arena of Aikido.

Kokyu Nage

The Author, Koichi Tohei

Performance of the Author at the General Headquarters Arena of Aikido.

CONTENTS

1

what is aikido?

There is no discord in the absolute truth of nature, but there is discord in the realm of relative truth Aikido is in accord with Nature.

WHAT IS AIKIDO?

THE principles of Aikido, most modern of Japan's martial arts, were discovered by Morihei Uyeshiba.

Its outstanding feature is that it made a great leap from the traditional physical arts to a spiritual martial art, from a relative martial art to an absolute art, from the aggressive, fighting martial arts to a spiritual martial art that seeks to abolish conflict.

When any one speaks of "myself," he nearly always means "my physical self, or existence." He knows that his body has weight and shape. Through his five senses of sight, smell, taste, hearing and touch, he is always conscious of his physical self. By contrast, his mind has neither color nor form. We wash our faces each morning, but how many of us wash our minds as well? Precious few! There are many people who train their bodies but few who train their minds. Apparently few realize that the mind like the body becomes soiled if it is not washed, weak if it is not trained.

Another important fact to remember is that actually the mind rules the body. It is the mind that leads and the body that follows. Aikido realizes this truth and teaches that before you attempt to move your body, you must use your mind, and when you are trying to throw your opponent, before you move his body, first lead his mind. Try to throw your opponent by brute force alone and you will find it heavy going. Remember that the mind has neither weight nor volume, that a big man does not necessarily have a heavy mind. If the art of leading the mind is learned and mastered, even a woman or a child can easily defeat a big man.

After seeing an Aikido exhibition for the first time, the usual reaction is to consider it a faked performance. "Common sense tells you it's all faked!" they say. The trouble with common sense is that it considers the body as its central figure and so derives only a half-knowledge of common sense, and cannot see the working of the mind. Only with a knowledge of the working of both mind and body can one know the truth. Then for the first time will Aikido's art be grasped. Arguing the point is useless; the only way to understand Aikido is to get down to real practice.

In most martial arts, an enemy is put up and the training is aimed at learning to defeat him. In Aikido, the aim is not to conquer the enemy but to conquer oneself. This is why Aikido is said to have leaped from the material, physical martial arts to a spiritual martial art.

Heaven and earth are one. Mastering any one of the martial arts means obedience to the absolute laws of Heaven and earth, or Nature. If you can truly understand and obey the laws of Nature and carry out her dictates, you become an integral part of Nature and any one who attacks you will be attacking Nature herself. There is no one who can hope to prevail against Nature's laws. To defeat an opponent is a relative victory. There is always a day coming when the victor of today becomes the vanquished of tomorrow. Become then a part of Nature; strive to grow in it and with it. Men of old said, "Do not blame others nor hate them. Be afraid only of your lack of sincerity." In Aikido, seek not to be strong but to be just, nor victory over an enemy but victory over self through correct principles.

Then if you can add polish to polish in your art, there will be no need to strive unduly to defeat an opponent. He himself will obey you and you will find yourself without an enemy. And you will understand then that Aikido has indeed made the leap from a physical martial art to a spiritual martial art.

The world today is full of conflict and this has led us to the brink of annihilation.

Conflict will never cease so long as mankind is convinced that this is a world of conflict and that any one who refuses to fight loses social status. If we sincerely wish for world peace, each individual must nurture within himself the spirit of non-aggression.

In Aikido, every art was designed in obedience to the laws of Nature so that there is no strain in its execution. Obey the laws of Nature in all your movements and win; disobey and lose. Let your opponent go where he wants to go; let him return where he wants to return and bend in the direction he wants to bend as you lead him, and then let him fall where he wants to fall. There is no need to strain yourself unduly.

You can try to turn back a stream, but you will have to use brute force to do it. How much easier it is to honor the power of the stream and lead it wherever you wish.

Again if a rock weighing 100 pounds is falling directly toward your head, it would be a tremendous feat to stop it with your bare hands. But if instead of trying to catch it, you step nimbly aside, the rock drops to the ground without doing you any harm. If the rock weighed 1,000 pounds, it would be just as easy to step aside. There is a limit to what you can accomplish by physical force, but what you can accomplish by non-violence is limitless. In Aikido, there is no practice in the use of brute force but there is training in how to use an opponent's own strength in leading him. To the degree that the feeling of contention disappears, your technique progresses. Women, children and older men may practice the Aikido arts easily and develop amazing strength.

For this reason, Aikido can call itself "the non-fighting martial art."

Aikido is not merely an art of self-defense but into its techniques and movements are woven elements of philosophy, psychology and dynamics. As you learn the various arts, you will at the same time train your mind, improve your health and develop an unbreakable self-confidence.

Today Aikido is spreading rapidly to all parts of the world because people everywhere seem to be able to understand and puts it principles into practice. I shall count myself fortunate if this book serves to lead those who wish to study Aikido into taking the first step by registering at a *dojo*.

2

principles of *ki*

Be warned against self-conceit. Know that it is brought on by shallow thinking and cheaply bought compromise with your ideals, although Nature is boundless.

Principles of KI

HE who would learn Aikido must first know. To go through the motions of Aikido without knowing *Ki* is like a dish prepared without seasoning: it has form and appearance but is neither salty nor sweet. There can be no true understanding of Aikido without *Ki*.

The name Aikido itself means the way of coordinating with *Ki*, and in daily Aikido practice, such expressions as, "pour forth *Ki*," "leading your opponent's *Ki*," "do not draw your *Ki* inward," or "do not stop the flow of *Ki*," are used constantly.

In Oriental thought, the idea of *Ki* is not difficult to understand, but in the English language, the equivalent word is hard to discover. It begins with the *Ki* of all nature and permeates our daily lives right down to the veriest trifle.

Let us here take up the principles of *Ki*.

The sun has been burning for a long, long time. If it is burning now, it must have begun burning at a certain time. If we are asked, what was there before that, we can answer only that there was nothing there. Now we know that something cannot come out of nothing. We must conclude that although there was seemingly nothing there, there must have been indications of the presence of something from which came the sun. The same way with the earth, the moon and stars.

In the beginning, the heavens and the earth must have been in a state of extreme fluidity, without color or form. There was nothing there yet there was something there, you might say. This state we call *Ki*. Many call it God; others call it Buddha, and still others by other names depending on where they live.

Take a piece of some substance and divide it into two. Continue dividing the halves into two indefinitely. Theoretically, you can continue the process and you will never reach zero. There will always be something to cut into two. 0×1 equals 0. 0×100 equals 0. If you reach zero, there is no way to return to your original 1. But as long as there is that submicroscopic piece of matter that is almost but not quite nothing, there is the possibility that it can join endlessly with like submicroscopic pieces of matter to form something. If we accept this line of reasoning, we can accept the theory that the heavens and the earth were formed by the endless joining together of infinitesimally tiny pieces of matter.

Whence came man? He was born of human parents. If we continue to ask, "And before that?" "And before that?" we conclude that man, too, is part of the creative process of the universe, the endless joining together of infinitesimally tiny pieces of matter.

So we call this state *Ki*. And the heavens and the earth, man and all substance of every kind was born of *Ki*, and returns to *Ki*. Even if it did not return to *Ki*, in itself it is part of the universal *Ki*. We might say that man himself is a mass of *Ki* surrounded by his body. It is as though a man in the ocean surrounds water with his arms and says, "This is my water." Since he has surrounded the water with his arms, he may be right about owning the water but from the viewpoint of the water, it is always in a state of fluidity and it is the ocean's water. Man might claim that he is leading his own life yet it is well for him to remember that his life is a part of the universal life.

If this truth becomes truly a part of a man's conscious being, then only can he claim to be at one with the universal *Ki*, and then only will he have attained the eternal life that is beyond mortal life and death.

So long as a man is alive, he must continue to receive universal *Ki* in a smooth, ever-flowing stream. When *Ki* flows smoothly, you feel alive and strong. When it is sluggish, you begin to feel indisposed and even ill. As the flow of *Ki* becomes progressively more sluggish and finally ceases altogether, the body faces death and disintegration.

One who receives universal *Ki* and lives can improve the stream of *Ki* he receives by himself sending out *Ki* into the universe. This keeps up the constant intake and outflow of *Ki*. In Aikido, the training at all times stresses the pouring forth of *Ki*, never of drawing it in or stopping its flow. Let your *Ki* flow out at all times and you will not only be active but your health will improve and you will feel alive and grow stronger.

How does one bring forth *Ki*?

Since one's own *Ki* is part of the universal *Ki*, one has only to let nature take its course, allowing *Ki* to flow constantly in and out, so that one's *Ki* is at one with that of the universe. This sounds simple but we have all become so accustomed to stopping our *Ki* or pulling our *Ki* in that it is extremely difficult to let nature take its course. It becomes necessary to change our habits so that we may at all times be able to pour forth *Ki* at will.

Here is one way to pour forth your *Ki*.

A makes a fist, puts strength into his arm and bends his elbow slightly. B uses both hands to try to bend A's arm. (B must always try to bend the arm in the way that the arm naturally bends at the elbow. If he tries to bend the arm in the wrong way, he might hurt A.)

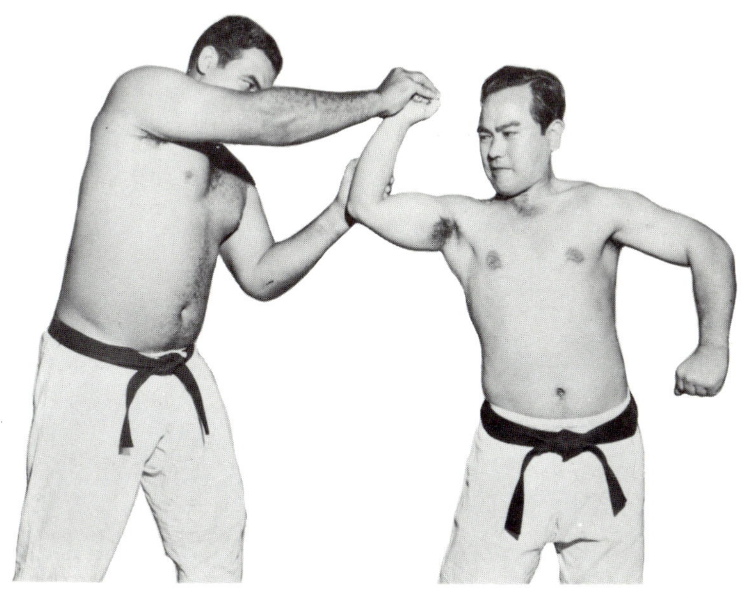

FIG. 1

Since A's arm is already slightly bent, if B's strength is equal to or greater than A's, he should not have much difficulty bending A's arm.

Next A takes the same position, this time opening his hand instead of making a fist and does not put any strength into his arm, but thinks of his arm as a fireman's hose through which his mind is flowing with great force as though his mind power were reaching for the ends of the universe. As long as this stream of thought is not cut, it does not matter how strong B is. He cannot bend A' arm.

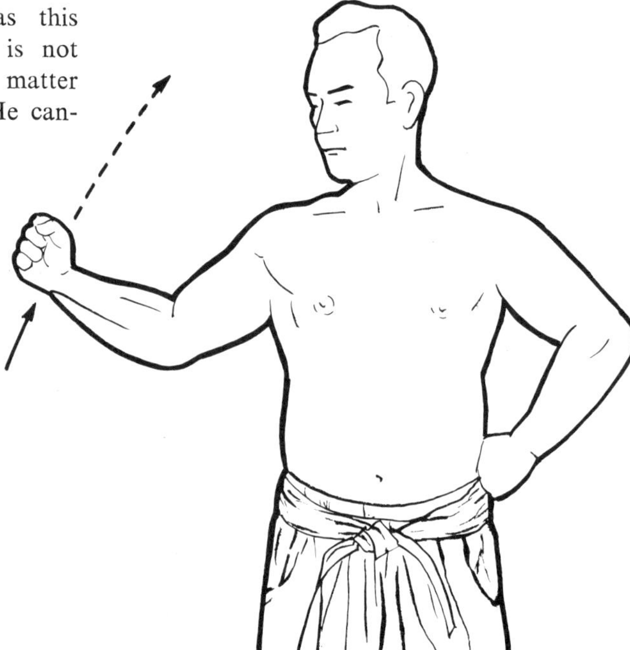

FIG. 2

Instead of arguing this point, prove or disprove it by action. Discover what great strength A has. But A must not doubt himself while he is proving his strength. Belief is power. Because he believes and acts as he believes, strength comes to him from his mind and he becomes stronger. Because the strength of the mind is directed in the same direction that the hand is pointing, there is coordination of mind and body. When the mind and body are coordinated, *Ki* manifests itself. Aikido calls this "pouring forth *Ki*." Any such feeling as, "I'm afraid I can't do it," and the like, Aikido calls "drawing *Ki* in."

As sound has sound waves and light has light waves, it stands to reason that the human mind as it controls our bodily movements should have mind waves. The mind is truly a source of power. Believe that power is emanating from your mind and power will be streaming out. So in Aikido practice, when you are told, "Pour out *Ki*," just believe positively, "My *Ki* is pouring out!"

Everyone has had some experiences which prove that when mind and body are fully coordinated, great power is engendered. "Fire! Fire!" you hear. You rush into the building and lift heavy objects that you could never have lifted, and carry them out of the house. Later when it is all over, you find that you no longer have the strength to carry these same objects back again.

On the battlefield, with bullets flying around you, you drink filthy water with impunity. Yet that same water drunk under ordinary circumstances will put you flat on your back.

If some fearful animal chased you, you could jump over a ditch so wide you would turn aside at any other time.

Where does this super-power came from? The answer is that you had it in you all the time. In an emergency, your mind works swiftly and joins its strength to that of physical power. In other words, you use power that comes from coordination of mind and body.

Although we all have this latent power, we not only do not know how to utilize it, we have even forgotten that we ever had it. This power that we can use effectively when mind and body are coordinated gives us great strength and enables us to use our maximum strength and makes life worth while and complete.

In Aikido, train at all times to coordinate mind and body in keeping your *Ki* flowing out until it becomes second nature with you. You will then be at one with nature in every pose and stance and your coordinated strength can be applied freely at any time and any place. You will be amazed at the strength you develop and the confidence with which you can face up to life's responsibilities.

3

the one point

Cultivate the calm mind that comes from putting nature into your body. Concentrate your thoughts on the one point.

Nearly every one when faced with an important occasion easily becomes tense with nervousness. When anyone must make a speech before a large audience for the first time, he becomes tense; his mind refuses to work and he often finds afterwards that he cannot remember what he said. Even a trained athlete becomes nervous just before an important game or match and not only is unable to exert his full strengh but makes unexpected errors. So in every field, the experienced ones say, "Relax!" Actually, unless you relax, your body cannot move quickly and your mind does not function.

In order to relax, you draw your strength out of your body but when you do so, somehow you feel undependable and weak so that on important occasions you begin to worry and cannot relax. You must know how to relax and yet not draw out your strength and feel weak but instead to be able to exert great strength.

Here it becomes necessary to understand the use of *Ki*. As explained in the examples of the bending of the arms, even if you are relaxed, as long as your *Ki* is flowing out, you can exert great strength. In other words, in order to relax, it is imperative that you keep pouring forth your *Ki*. As long as there is an outpouring of *Ki*, you can maintain a posture of strength and still move swiftly in any direction, so you can relax without worry.

Next comes the problem of where to put the strength that we have drained from the body in relaxing. We must order this strength to go and settle somewhere. This settling place is The One Point Below The Navel, or a point two fingers or so below the navel, the center of the lower abdomen.

THE ONE POINT

Every object has its center of gravity near the bottom. Even a human being must be considered to be an object. When it is allowed to stand naturally, its center of gravity should be at The One Point.

If the mind is relaxed and concentrated here, and the rest of your body drained of its strength, then comes true relaxation.

Example One: As shown in Figure 3, A and B, place their hands back to back and push against each other. A concentrates his mind on The One Point and is relaxed, sending his *Ki* forward powerfully along his arm. No matter how much B strains to push A back, A can ignore his efforts and B cannot succeed in pushing A back. On the contrary, A has only to keep on walking forward and the only thing B can do is retreat.

FIG. 3

FIG. 4

Example Two: A takes a half step forward and fully bends his body backward, concentrating his mind on The One Point, withdrawing the strength from his upper body.

B tries to force A's shoulder down but as long as A keeps his mind on The One Point, B cannot do so. It is easy to see how much strength A has.

Next A puts his strength into his shoulder and B throws him down easily.

There are any number of other examples that can be given but briefly the important lesson to learn is that if you keep your center of gravity at The One Point as you train, you can relax. You can see that to put strength into your head and throw it back or swagger about with your shoulders perked up is unnatural.

It is easy to make a mistake about one important point. When The One Point is mentioned, many concentrate their physical strength there. When this is done, strength naturally goes also to the torso and The One Point is forgotten. The One Point is not the place to concentrate your physical strength but the place for your mind to settle.

"This is the center of my mind," is all you need to think of The One Point. Once you have learned to attain this state of mind, use it in your daily training and practice using it in all your actions. Since this state of mind allows your center of gravity to rest where it should, constant practice soon enables you without conscious effort to get the habit of relaxing at all times, able to use the potential of your mind and body at a moment's notice.

To be able to pour forth your *Ki*, you must always settle your mind on The One Point. If you do not, you cannot pour forth your *Ki*. To put it another way, when your *Ki* is pouring out, it is always when your mind is settled on The One Point. These two sentences sound different but they are exactly the same in meaning. Thus Aikido training can be carried on anywhere at any time.

When something serious happens, if you ask yourself, "Is my inner self on The One Point?" and make certain that the answer is, "Yes !" you have no reason to become excited but can remain calm and relaxed. If you become angry, you know that The One Point is gone and you immediately relax and remind yourself that your mind must be on The One Point, and your anger disappears before you are aware of it. Whether you walk or drive, if your mind is on The One Point, you feel no fatigue. So day by day, moment by moment, you live life usefully, polishing your own character.

The *dojo* is a place to study the theory of truth, to test whether one's daily actions have been right, to ascertain whether one has gained any strength, and further to polish one's art. As we look into a mirror and correct our bad points, so we can see whether or not we are correct by seeing how our opponents act.

The Aikido arts are so designed that if you act correctly, you can always throw your opponent. If you find it impossible to throw him, there is a flaw in your execution, and it is time to review the fundamentals and seek the advice of your instructor.

Study and master also the 1,000 changes and 10,000 variations of Aikido. Strive to maintain the attitude of strength at all times; be calm and relaxed. In this way, you learn to conquer not your opponent but yourself.

4

the arts of aikido

The martial arts begin with courtesy and end with courtesy, not in form alone but in heart and mind as well.

THE ARTS OF AIKIDO

Do not criticize any of the other martial arts. Speak ill of others and it will surely come back to you. The mountain does not laugh at the river because it is lowly, nor does the river speak ill of the mountain because it cannot move about.

IF classified in detail, there are more than 10,000 arts in Aikido. It would be impossible to explain them one by one. So I have grouped the arts into several categories according to the methods used by an opponent in attacking. Instead of learning to counter-attack, you will learn how to lead and throw or subdue an opponent.

1. Ude Furi Undo
   Ude Furi Choyaku Undo
2. Katate Tori Shiho Nage
   (A) Irimi
   (B) Tenkan
3. Katate Tori Kokyu Nage
4. Katate Tori Ryote Mochi Kokyu Nage
5. Ryote Tori Kokyu Nage
6. Kata Tori Nikyo
7. Mune Tsuki Kote Gaeshi
8. Shomen Uchi Kokyu Nage
9. Yokomen Uchi Shiho Nage
10. Ushiro Tori Kokyu Nage
11. Ushiro Kata Tori Kote Gaeshi
12. Ushiro Katate Tori Kubi Shime Sankyo

1. Ude Furi Undo

This exercise is based on the largest number of Aikido arts, so before beginning your training, practice this exercise and become thoroughly familiar with its movements.

Stand erect. Concentrate your thoughts on The One Point, and keep the whole body relaxed.

Count One. Keeping your upper body and head facing the front, your fingers spread apart, swing your arms wide to the left (Fig. 5).

FIG. 5

Count Two. Swing your arms to the right (Fig. 6).

Imagine a steel rod down the middle of your body. Even when you swing your arms, the body must not bend. If the steel rod is kept straight, when swinging your arms to left or right, no matter whether your hips be pushed from the left or right, you will not be moved. But if that steel rod is missing, you become very weak. When swinging your arms, if you put strength into them, you are pulled by the strength of your arms and there is no steel rod down the middle, and your body is swayed. You will need to relax and let your *Ki* pour out fully. Swing your arms as though you were trying to start a wind with your finger tips.

FIG. 6

Next, at Count One, start as in Figure 7 and, while swinging your arms to the left, step forward with the right foot, turn your body to the left, the left foot following this action by facing backward (Fig. 7).

FIG. 7

At Count Two, swing your arms to the right, at the same time turning your body around to the right. Your body returns to the former position, facing forward (Fig. 8).

Practice this repeatedly.

Begin in slow motion, then increase the tempo as the count goes faster. Do not think so much about what your body is doing as about creating a whirlwind by your action.

By the working of your powerful *Ki,* you suck your opponent no matter how strong he may be into the vortex of your power and throw him.

FIG. 8

2. Katate Tori Shiho Nage

A. Irimi

Uke assumes the *migi hanmi* (45° angle to the right) position and grasps *Nage's* wrist.

Nage: Assume the same *migi hanmi* position as *Uke* and let him grasp your left wrist. Right here, it is well to note the great difference it makes in the power of your *Ki* whether you think, "He is holding my wrist," or, "I am letting him hold my wrist."

Nage: Pour out your *Ki* fully along your left arm, and with unbendable arm, turn your fingertips a little to the right. At this point, be sure that your wrist is not straining against *Uke's* strength.

FIG. 9

Then when you move your body closer to *Uke,* your left arm, pushed by *Uke's* right arm, will assume the position shown in Figures 10 and 11. You will find that you cannot accomplish the same result if you try to do it by using the strength of your left arm to force *Uke's* right arm. By bringing your hips close to *Uke* you are making use of his pushing power, adding his power to yours.

FIG. 10

FIG. 11

Nage: Next, with your right hand. grasp *Uke's* right hand lightly from the outside, step in front of him lightly with your left foot (Fig. 12), at the same time lifting both arms, pivot fully to the right (Fig. 13), and bring your arms down smartly to bring *Uke* down on his back.

FIG. 12

FIG. 13

In Figure 13, if you turn your body fully to the right, *Uke* will fall, and it may not be necessary to bring your arm down since the force of your turning will do the trick. When you grasp *Uke's* right wrist with your right hand, it is important that you do so lightly, continuing to pour forth *Ki* along your left arm so that your own strength will not be in your way.

FIG. 14

B. Tenkan

Uke assumes the right *hanmi* position, and grasps *Nage's* left hand (Fig. 14).

Nage: Assume the left *hanmi* position and let *Uke* grasp your left hand. The movements of your hands and upper body are the same as in *Irimi* but in this movement your left foot is already in front of *Uke,* so you will not be able to advance it any farther.

If you did advance it, your posture will become unbalanced. Turn your body to the right and bring your right foot around backward and plant it firmly as close to *Uke* as possible (Figs. 15 and 16).

FIG. 15

FIG. 16

Then twist your hips sharply to the right and *Uke* will fall backward (Figs. 17, 18). In this way, you can throw your opponent in any direction by using your hips and feet. Thus the name *Shiho Nage* (all directions throw). The movements of your feet in *Irimi* and *Tenkan* are the basic movements of all the Aikido arts. Practice your foot work without moving the position of the wrist that *Uke* is holding and it will enable you to execute the *Irimi* and *Tenkan* arts, starting with your feet in any position.

This is the way with all the Aikido arts, but of prime importance is to practice with your opponent holding you so that you may get the feel of various forces working for or against you. Once you reach this point, further practice will consist of gradually learning how to respond instantly when *Uke's* hand touches any part of you.

FIG. 17

FIG. 18

3. Katate Tori Kokyu Nage

Nage: In Katate Tori Shiho Nage, you let *Uke* hold your left hand but this time you assume the *migi hanmi* (45° angle to the right), and let *Uke* grasp your right hand with his own right hand (Fig. 19).

FIG. 19

Nage: As you learned in *Ude Furi Choyaku Undo,* make a full swing with your left arm, aiming to grasp *Uke's* neck. Take a step forward with your left foot toward *Uke's* right rear, and at the same time grasp the back of his neck lightly (Fig. 20). Lead him toward your right with your right arm and step around with your right foot to *Uke's* rear.

FIG. 20

Nage: Uke's posture is crumbling. His right arm is stretched as far as it can go. Keep your hold on the nape of his neck; bring back your right arm. Turn your hips to the left. Take a step with your right foot toward *Uke's* right rear and at the same time push his neck down and throw him with your bent right arm. (Fig. 21). As you push *Uke's* neck down, make sure that your arm is bent and your fingertips are pointing downward. Don't loosen your grip on his neck until you start to push him downward. If you do, he will straighten up and give you trouble in throwing him. Do not stop the flow of *Ki* for even an instant.

FIG. 21

When you have reached the point of Figure 20, do not draw in your *Ki* from your right arm. If you do, *Uke's* arm will become too strong for you to bring it around to the back. Stretch your arm as far as it will go and then, using centrifugal force, bring back his arm without straining against his strength.

If the principle of the swing is used, and you swing *Uke's* right arm, that arm will swing back automatically and you should have no difficulty in throwing him down (Fig. 23).

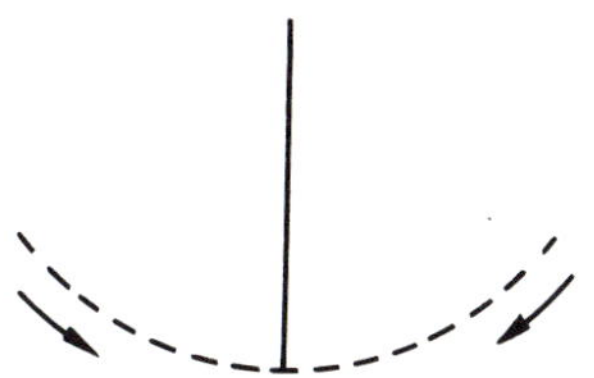

FIG. 22

FIG. 23

4. Katate Tori Ryote Mochi Kokyu Nage

Uke holds *Nage's* right hand with both hands.

Nage: You can throw *Uke* just as easily as when *Uke* was holding your hand with his right hand. He can hold your hand more firmly with both hands, but when you pour enough *Ki* into your right arm and leap in to grasp *Uke's* neck, you can throw him just as easily as you do in *Katate Tori Kokyu Nage.* Learn how to avoid clashing with *Uke's* power.

FIG. 24

5. Ryote Tori Kokyu Nage

Uke holds *Nage's* hands (Fig. 25).

Nage: If *Uke* is stronger than you, it is difficult to move him. Pour forth your *Ki* freely and stop straining your arms.

FIG. 25

Step backward slowly with the left foot, at the same time turning your hips a little to the left (Fig. 26). You have moved your body backward without moving the position of your wrist, so your left arm must be stretched taut. This is important.

FIG. 26

Swing your hips farther to the left, and when *Uke* totters forward, grasp his right wrist lightly and throw him in the direction he is tottering (Fig. 27).

FIG. 27

At the point of Figure 25, until your arms become stretched, move your hips so that it will not be noticed. Keep your arms stretched but do not pull *Uke's* arms. If your arms are not fully stretched, your next movement will be a complete waste. And if you pull his arms, he will pull back. If your arms are not taut, you cannot even twist your hips in the next movement.

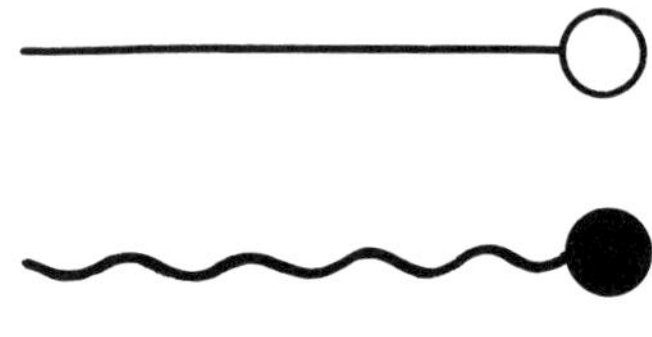

FIG. 28

In the drawing above there is a cannon ball and attached to it is a cord. Jerk the cord with all your strength when it is lying limp, and your strength will be wasted. But when the cord is taut, the cannon ball will answer your jerk and will come rolling into your hands. The cord is your arms, the cannon ball your opponent. Use this principle and you can easily throw an opponent no matter how much bigger and stronger than you. Always remember that your strength comes from The One Point.

6. Kata Tori Nikyo (Nikajo)

Uke's assumes the right *hanmi* position and tries to grasp *Nage's* left shoulder.

Nage: A split second before *Uke's* hand touches your shoulder, step backward with your left foot and turn your hips to the left. Stretch *Uke's* right arm so that he will be led to you, and grasp his right wrist. Your little finger must be put firmly on *Uke's* little finger from the outside of his hand (Figs. 29 and 30).

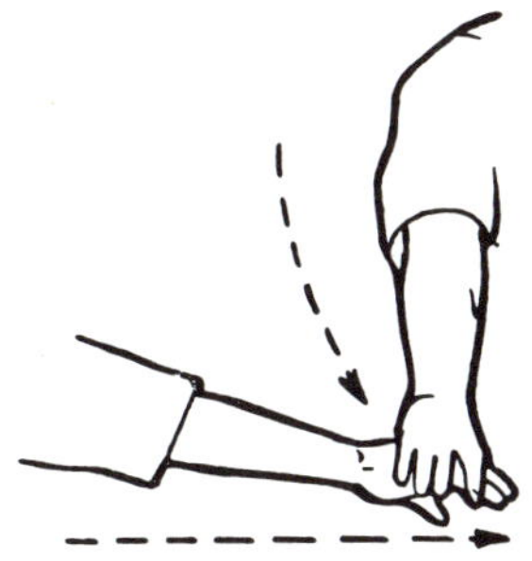

FIG. 29

FIG. 30

And immediately push his arm back toward his head (Fig. 31).

FIG. 31

Uke's posture crumbles, so he will try to right himself. Draw his right elbow toward you with your left hand and bend his arm. Clamp his right wrist with both hands. At this moment, *Uke's* right arm is in the shape of the letter Z. Bring his wrist down toward the center of his body. *Uke,* unable to bear the pain in his wrist, will collapse. At this moment, put your left hand on *Uke's* right elbow and with both hands, push *Uke's* right arm down in front of him (Fig. 33).

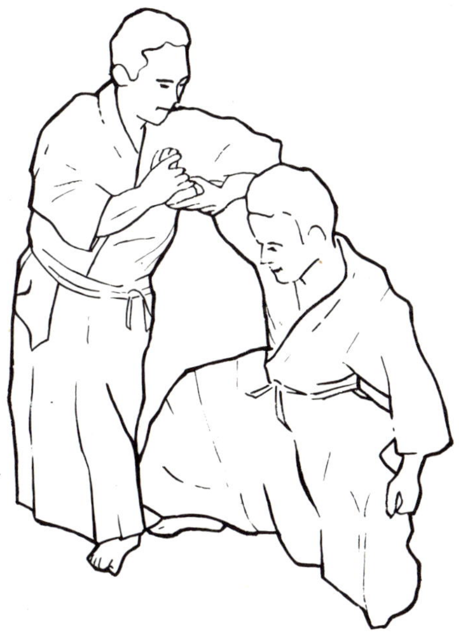

FIG. 32

Lift *Uke's* right wrist up, and while moving your body sideways, clamp his right wrist in your left arm. Push *Uke's* right shoulder down with your right hand and then push him down with your whole body, *Uke* will surrender (Fig. 34).

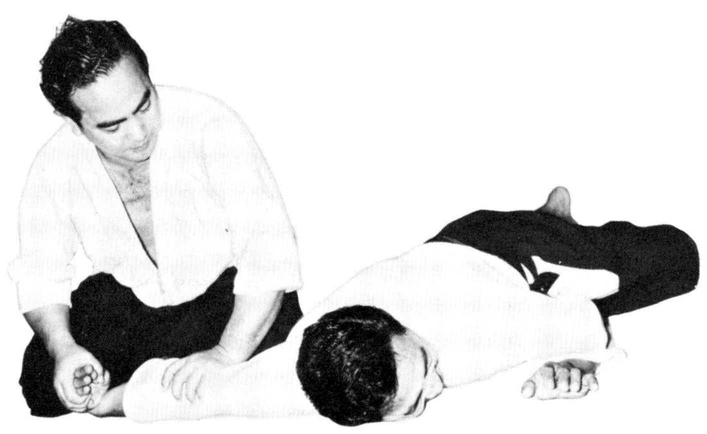

FIG. 33

In Aikido, you always push your opponent down on his stomach. If you push him down on his back, he will resist and attack you with his arms and legs. If he is lying on his stomach, he is unable to make a single move that will be of any use.

It is enough to push him down at any one point to keep him quiet. One thing you must remember in this art is to stretch *Uke's* right arm fully when you grasp his right wrist. If his arm is not stretched fully, it will become quite difficult to push it back in Figure 32. And in pushing his arm back, you can use your left hand too. Ram his right arm back, and the rest is easy.

And in Figure 33, bring your arms down with a single movement. Don't put unnecessary strength into it or your strength will work against you.

FIG. 34

7. Mune Tsuki Kote Gaeshi

Uke throws a punch at *Nage's* chest in a stabbing motion.

Nage: Your position is that of left *hanmi.* Turn your hips to the right and, an instant before *Uke's* fist hits your chest, turn your right foot to the right and at the same time take one step backward. Your left arm is stretched in the direction of *Uke's* punch. You grasp *Uke's* right wrist (Fig. 35 and 36), and lead *Uke's* body in a large circular movement, making use of centrifugal force.

FIG. 35

Fig. 36

Nage: Thrust *Uke's* wrist back to the left with your left arm (Fig. 37), and with both hands, ram his wrist downward. He will tumble over to your left (Fig. 38).

FIG. 37

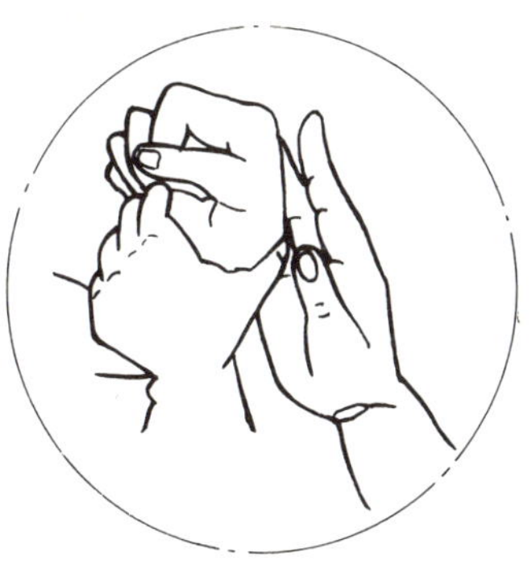

FIG. 38

In Figure 35, you grasp his wrist but do not stop the momentum of his arm. Stop it and he will be ready to attack you with the left arm and legs. Stretch his arm in the direction of the thrust, and he will totter as he loses his balance. At this moment, you turn to the right and *Uke* can do nothing but follow your body, making a big turn to the right. When he stops turning, ram his wrist back, and he will fall.

The important thing is to continue the flow of your movement. Exact timing plays a large part in all arts of Aikido.

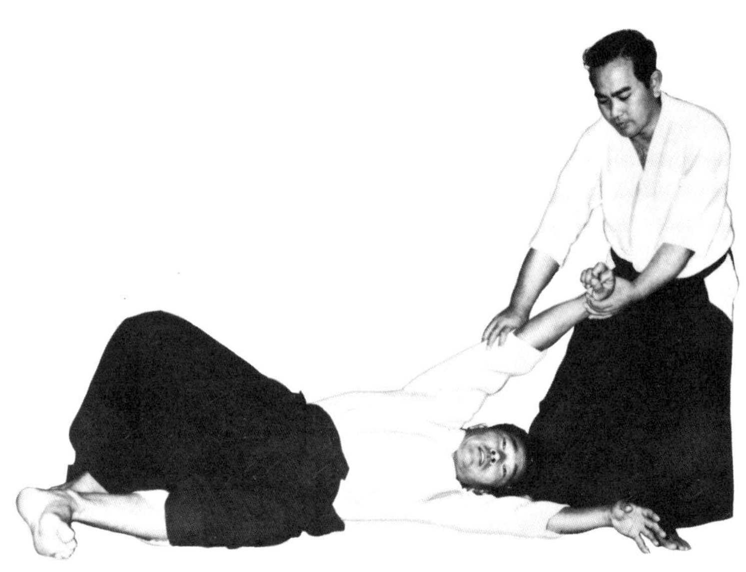

FIG. 39

Nage: The instant *Uke* falls down, put your right hand on the outside of his elbow, and walk once around his head and he will be facing downward (Fig. 39 and 40).

Push him down in the same manner as in *Kata Tori Nikyo.* When you roll him over, make sure his right arm is always stretched taut. It makes it easier to make him face downward.

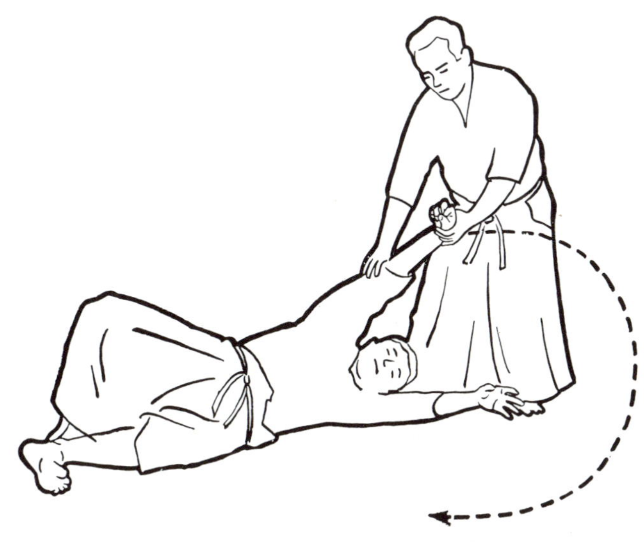

FIG. 40

8. Shomen Uchi Kokyu Nage

Uke's body is in the right *hanmi* position. He strikes at *Nage's* forehead with his right hand.

Nage: Assume the right *hanmi* position. Pour forth *Ki* into your right arm, and the instant *Uke's* arm comes down to your forehead, thrust your arm out in the direction of the dotted line in Figure 41.

FIG. 41

Just as you strike *Uke's* right arm down from the outside, step deep into *Uke's* right rear, and at the same time grab him by the neck with your left hand. Without stopping the flow of your movement, turn your hips farther to the right, and step to your right with your right foot. Push *Uke's* wrist down with your right hand. With the left hand, push his neck down (Fig. 42).

FIG. 42

Nage: Uke will try to stand erect. Use this strength of his. Pour forth *Ki* into your right arm. Release *Uke's* wrist, and in the same movement, put your right arm around his neck. Twist your body to the left. Step in back of *Uke* with the right foot. Using your right foot for leverage, push him down with your right shoulder and arm. Pour forth your *Ki* as though you were going to bury your fingertips into the ground. The movement of your right arm will follow the dotted line shown in Figure 43 and 44.

FIG. 43

Release his neck only the instant before he falls down. If you do this too soon, *Uke* will find a chance to regain his stance, and the flow of your movement will be cut off. As in *Ude Furi Choyaku Undo*, your arms must move in the same direction.

In Figure 41, if you draw in your *Ki* from the right arm, *Uke* will push it down easily. You will not be able to leap to his right side. Pour forth *Ki* from the right arm, and *Uke's* right arm will slide down the outer side of your right arm.

In Figure 42, you see the application of the principle of the swing. Stretch his right arm down as far as it can go and you can use his strength when he tries to draw it up.

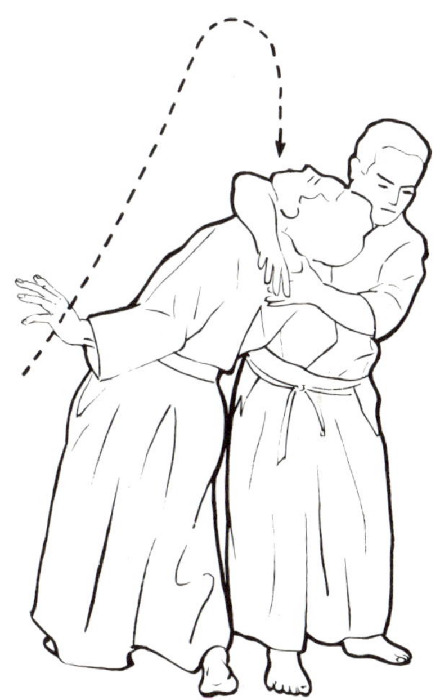

FIG. 44

9. Yoko Men Uchi Shiho Nage

Uke: With his body in the right ***hanmi*** position strikes at the left side of *Nage's* face.

Nage: Assume the left ***hanmi*** position. Turn your face a little to the right. Make it easy for *Uke* to strike you.

FIG. 45

The instant he strikes, put *Ki* into your left arm and thrust it up as though to graze the right side of his face from below. Do not try to stop *Uke's* right arm (Fig. 45). Twist your body to the left and step backward with the left foot. Strike down on *Uke's* right wrist and grasp it with both hands (Fig. 46).

FIG. 46

Without stopping the flow of *Uke's* strength, lift up his arm in the direction of the arrow in Figure 48, and step forward in front of *Uke* with the left foot.

FIG. 47

Lifting up his right arm over your forehead, turn your body fully to the right. *Uke* will fall on his back (Fig. 48).

After stepping forward in front of *Uke* with the left foot in Figure 49, the throw that follows is the same as in *Katate Tori Shiho Nage.* The only difference is that you are holding *Uke's* right hand with both of your hands.

FIG. 48

In Figure 47, if you try to stop *Uke's* right arm with your left hand, *Uke's* strength will work against you and you will not be able to move your body backward. Pour forth your *Ki* toward *Uke's* face. Step out of the arc *Uke* makes and you can grasp his right hand easily. It will become easy to throw him off balance. Don't put unnecessary strength into your left hand in grasping his right arm or you will stop his momentum and that means straining against his power. Grasp his arm lightly with plenty of *Ki* pouring forth into your arms.

FIG. 49

10. Ushiro Tori Kokyu Nage

Uke hugs *Nage* from behind over his arms. (Fig. 50)

Nage: Stretch your arms straight down and let *Uke* hug you. Pour forth *Ki* from your arms and with unbendable arm slide them toward the front of your body in the direction indicated in Figures 51 and 52.

FIG. 50

Fig. 51

Fig. 52

When *Uke* tries to tighten his hug, stretch both arms toward the sides and then, forward. Take one step forward with the left foot (Fig. 53).

Fig. 53

Stretch the left arm down to the ground and drop the left shoulder. With the same movement, swing the right arm up and to the rear. Turn your hips forcefully to the right. *Uke* will make a turn in the air and fall in front of you (Fig. 54).

In Figure 53, it will not do you any good if you try to lift up your arms or loosen *Uke's* hug. If *Uke* is strong enough, you cannot even move your shoulders. *Uke's* strength is working in the direction of the two bent arrows so you will have to lead his strength farther to the front.

Slide your arms forward, and then stretch them to the side. *Uke's* upper body is on your back, and a twist of your hips will be enough to throw him. When your arms are stretched downward, pour forth *Ki* in that direction. In Figure 54, make *Uke* slide down your arms, your back and then the left arm. Just as his center of gravity shifts downward, swing the right arm up and backward and throw him.

FIG. 54

11. Ushiro Kata Tori Kote Gaeshi

Uke grasps *Nage's* shoulders from behind.

Nage: Do not let your mind center on your back nor let your center of gravity be disturbed but concentrate on The One Point (Fig. 55).

FIG. 55

Swing your arms up over your head and lead *Uke's* strength upward. At the same time, step backward with the left foot to the outside of *Uke's* left foot (Fig. 56).

FIG. 56

Keep your posture straight and do not move your shoulders. If you put strength into your shoulders, you are straining against *Uke's* power and you will be unable to make the next move. Step lightly backward with the left foot without moving the upper body. Bend your upper body down suddenly. Bend your left knee and drop your hips. Step backward with your right foot to *Uke's* left rear (Fig. 57).

FIG. 57

Lift up your head through *Uke's* arms. Grasp his right arm and apply *Kote Gaeshi* with your left hand (Fig. 58) and throw him (Fig. 59).

The moment after you lift up your arms and lead *Uke's* strength upward in Figure 56, bend your body down (Fig. 57) and just when *Uke* totters forward, lift up your head. Your movements from Figure 55 to 58 must be in one smooth flow.

FIG. 58

When you are attacked from behind, your mind is easily attracted to the rear and your *Ki* is pulled back. Maintain your center of gravity, remain calm, and concentrate on The One Point. Pour your *Ki* in the direction you are facing so you can detect even the slightest movement of your opponent. Do not panic simply because you are attacked from behind. Pour forth your *Ki* forward, not backward. If you are facing forward, but letting your *Ki* flow backward, your stance is weak. Your mind and body are not coordinated at all.

Concentrate your attention in the direction you are facing. That means good coordination and you can keep a strong posture. You can move swiftly in any direction at any time.

There is no difference at all in being attacked from the rear or the front. The arts you use are the same.

FIG. 59

12. Ushiro Katate Tori Kubi Shime Sankyo

Uke holds *Nage's* left wrist from behind with his left hand, and with his right arm chokes *Nage* by the neck (Fig. 60).

Any one can figure that if *Nage* lifts his face, he is leaving his throat wide open and he will be choked. So *Nage* puts strength in his chin and resists *Uke*, but it will not do any good against *Uke's* power.

An object must have its center of gravity near its bottom. The gravitational center of your head is in the tip of your chin. The One Point is the center of your upper body. Do not shift your center of gravity. Do not shift your mind. Remain calm and do nothing, and *Uke* will find it hard to choke your throat.

FIG. 60

Nage: Bend your wrists fully to the inside. Pouring torth *Ki* into the wrists, cross your arms in front of your body. Grasp *Uke's* left hand with your right hand from the outside (Fig. 61).

FIG. 61

Lift *Uke's* left arm above your head in one swift movement. His left hand is still grasping your left hand (Fig. 62).

FIG. 62

Twist your body to the right, and as you step backward to *Uke's* left rear, bring your arms down swiftly (Fig. 63). The movement of your arms must follow the line indicated in Figure 64. At this moment *Uke* will release your neck.

FIG. 63

FIG. 64

Still holding *Uke's* left hand as shown in Figure 64, put your left hand on his elbow and lead him down in the direction of his left hand (Fig. 65).

FIG. 65

This way of holding your opponent's hand is called *Sankyo* (Fig. 66). The pain your opponent feels is intense, so you can control his whole body simply by grasping his hand in this way. You can lead him wherever you like. Hold his hand lightly, and the pain you inflict is not so bad, but if he resists, all his power will work against himself. This art is most suitable for policemen. Master this thoroughly and you can subdue your opponent easily if he attacks you from behind or strikes at you from behind or strikes at you from the front.

In Figure 62, even the slightest drawing in of *Ki* makes it impossible to cross your arms in front of you. *Uke's* strength will become too great for you to do it. Bend the wrist fully to the inside. Pour forth *Ki* and relax.

FIG. 66

THIS concludes the explanation of the fundamental arts of Aikido. In these techniques, I have explained the methods of application only after you have let your opponent grasp tightly or strike you. The movements you have learned are the very foundation of Aikido. After mastering these, train further to apply your arts swiftly the instant before your opponent touches your body.

When you are going to sit down in a chair, if someone pulls the chair from under you the moment your *Ki* touches the chair, you can do nothing but fall on your backside. Your *Ki* was led away along with the chair. We apply the same principle in Aikido. When somebody attacks you, his *Ki* is always flowing toward you. Grasp his *Ki* and lead it along. Don't stop it. His body will follow his *Ki*. Your opponent's body has weight and power. Struggling against this is quite a task, but his *Ki* has neither weight nor shape. It has its flow and nothing else. His *Ki* moves his body. So grasp his *Ki* and lead it along. Don't strain against it. Once you have learned to lead his *Ki*, you can control his body.

To know the flow of his *Ki* and lead it, you must train your own *Ki* and become able to use it freely. You are facing forward but your *Ki* is flowing backward. You are reading a book but your mind is somewhre else. You read the newspapers while eating breakfast. These are some of the instances in which you are forgetting the training of *Ki*. Turn your *Ki* in full to the meal, and you can really appreciate its taste. That is when it sticks to your ribs. Read with your *Ki* when you read a book. Don't just follow the words with your eyes. Concentrate all your attention on what you are doing at the moment. That is the training of *Ki*. If you put your mind to it, you can do the training anywhere, anytime. The *dojo* is not the only place for training. When you want to get angry, get angry. But remember to find out what makes you angry, and get rid of the cause. Maybe you had a hard time at the office, but don't take it out on your family.

Aikido is training not so much to defeat an opponent as it is to conquer yourself. Your opponent is not just one with whom you strive but a mirror to help you both correct your errors, a grindstone to sharpen your art. Before you try to use your opponent's *Ki* against himself, learn to use your own *Ki* fully. Your aim should be not just to defeat your opponent and become strong but to discipline yourself as you build up your character.

In the beginning, the whole subject of *Ki* may seem strange and difficult but continued practice using the correct techniques will bring understanding. Once this point is reached, the rest is study and training to enjoy the profound satisfaction of tasting the deeper truths of which there seem no end. Complete mastery of Aikido may not be attained but what joy there is in seeking that goal.

5

prof. morihei uyeshiba

As nature loves and protects all creation and helps all things grow and develop, AIKIDO leads every devotee along the straight and narrow path and strives to teach mankind its truths with all sincerity.

LET us suppose that there is a steep mountain as yet unconquered. Though many have tried to reach its summit, only a few have even reached half way. Some lost their way; some lost their lives, but many fortunately returned without mishap. Then came a man of iron will, intrepidity, determination and cool contemplation. With inflexible spirit and knowledge of the mountain based on the experience of his predecessors, he finally attained the summit through his supreme effort.

He spent a lifetime to reach this summit. Then he looked back and opened a way to others by the sign-posts he left behind. Today, anybody may climb this mountain without losing his way and may enjoy the same thrill he enjoyed.

If a trail-blazer had not shown the way to the summit, one who came later not only would be unable to climb the mountain but would be unable to judge whether or not the way he was walking was right or wrong. Who would not express his gratitude for what this trail-blazer had done?

We feel the same gratitude to one who blazes a trial for our lives. Many people worship Jesus Christ and others believe in Buddha, because they enjoy the benevolent influences of these great teachers.

It is the same in Aikido. Those who through Aikido wish to understand the laws of Nature and put them into practice must first express their gratitude for what Professor Uyeshiba has done and must engrave his name in their hearts. Therefore, I shall present a brief sketch of Professor Uyeshiba's life.

professor MORIHEI UYESHIBA

He was born in Wakayama Prefecture in Japan. In his childhood, he was sickly and weak, and nobody could have imagined his becoming a man of robust health and the founder of such a superior art which startled all Japan. He made up his mind to train his body through the martial arts. The originator of Aikido, in which spiritual discipline and mental training are highly regarded, at first like all the rest trained himself only on the physical level.

He practiced almost all the existing martial arts, beginning with *Kito-ryu Jujitsu, Yagyu-ryu, Aioi-ryu, Hozoin-ryu* and finally *Daito-ryu.* Whatever he thought was best, even modern gymnastics, *Judo, Kendo,* bayonet arts, he took up and studied at every opportunity. He wandered from place to place seeking teachers, and spent his inheritance in this way.

During his training period, he showed the utmost courtesy to his teachers, even preparing food for them. Once training started, he devoted himself completely to his task. In his adolescence, he was only five feet one inch tall yet weighed 165 pounds. His formerly weak body became as strong as iron. His undeviating determination was to devote himself to training so that he could triumph over all others.

During the Russo-Japanese War (1904-1905), he volunteered for service in the Japanese Army, fighting at the front and testing his own strength and his command over the arts. He then went to Hokkaido and worked as a foreman of the immigrants. Even while engaged in farming, his obsession was his training in the martial arts.

With only a *bokken* (wooden sword), he wandered all over Japan and if he found one superior to him, remained with him as a pupil and trained until he had learned all that he could learn from him, then moved on. He became the most proficient man in the martial arts in Japan. In fact, he was invincible.

However, just as he was about to accomplish his goal, some doubt grew in his mind, not on the individual arts themselves but rather on all martial arts in general. To throw others, to strike them down, to fight and prevail over them—of what use is it all, anyway? he asked. If this is all that the martial arts mean to us, of what value are they?

To win means that some day we shall lose. Today's victor will be the vanquished tomorrow.

You are physically strong in your youth, but your strength wanes with advancing age and a younger man will overcome you. Today you are in the prime of life and can enjoy the feeling that comes in overcoming others, but the time will surely come when you yourself will be overcome. Because others lose, you win. Such victories are relative. Is there such a thing as absolute victory?

Even though you are victorious, what does this do for you? In the eyes of Nature, to win or lose in the world of men looks valueless, of no more meaning than the ebb and flow of the waves on the shore. Was it not a waste of energy to put a lifetime of effort into such a thing?

You may subdue others; you may not be able to control your own mind. If you cannot control your mind at will, winning over others will not bring you happiness. Your vanity may be satisfied, but what benefit does this bring to mankind in general?

Once the doubt grew, it led to others and finally to endless doubts about everything. Professor Uyeshiba, once he starts anything, puts his whole soul into it until it is completed. This time he laid the martial arts aside and put his entire energy to resolving his doubts.

He knocked at the doors of famous temples and he studied philosophy. He went into solitude and meditated. He remained under a waterfall to open "The eyes of his soul." Determined to solve his problem, he continued his ascetic life. Alone on a mountain, swinging his wooden sword, he became absorbed in the question, "What is martial art?"

After some years of training and pilgrimages, he came down one day from a mountain, entered the yard of a cottage, poured water over his body and looked up into the blue sky. Suddenly at this moment he felt strangely inspired. He was uplifted, simply delighted as tears rolled down his cheeks in an expression of gratitude to heaven and earth. In a flash of light, he perceived the truth. He realized that he had became one with the Universe.

"Seek, and ye shall find." He sought the truth earnestly, and endeavored painstakingly to find the answer to his question and God willed that he should find it. At last, with mind and body, he experienced the great truth of Nature. Now he surrendered his small ego and made the spirit of Nature his own mind.

This may be called a revelation of God, a state of perception of the absolute truth, as *Zen* calls it.

Professor Uyeshiba, recalling the events of that day, always tells the story as follows:

"As I was strolling in the yard, the earth suddenly trembled. Golden vapor gushed out of the earth enveloping my body, and then I felt myself turning into a golden body. At the same time, my mind and body felt light; I could understand what the chirping birds were saying and I understood clearly the creator's spirit. It was precisely at that moment that I received enlightenment: the fundamental principle of the martial arts is God's love and universal love. Tears of ecstasy rolled down my cheeks. From that time on, I have felt that the entire earth is my home and the sun and stars are mine. Neither position, nor fame, nor honors, nor wealth, nor the desire to become more powerful than others have any attraction for me—these have all vanished

"The martial arts are not concerned with brute force to knock opponents down, nor with lethal weapons that lead the world into destruction. The true martial arts, without struggling, regulate the *Ki* of the universe, guard the peace of the world, and produce and bring to maturity everything in Nature.

"Therefore, martial training is not training that has as its primary purpose the defeating of others, but practice of God's love within ourselves."

Since then, Professor Uyeshiba has taken great pains to express this lofty feeling. He learned that it is impossible to reveal such a feeling of mind and body through the martial arts and other methods that existed at that time. Since he was trying to express the spirit of heaven and earth, there would have to be a new kind of arts which would be capable of manifesting the will of Nature.

Thus the martial arts practiced by Professor Uyeshiba changed from day to day and finally evolved into this new creation which is the Aikido of today.

The violent and fierce arts previously practiced, which crushed everything changed into gentle, harmonious arts, which tenderly embraced all things. Professor Uyeshiba moves with grace as though he were performing a Japanese dance, seemingly oblivious of the existence of his opponent. He throws in a second several strong men and yet those who are thrown do not know how it was done. His every movement is in accord with the laws of Nature, and the power of the opponent who leaps at him goes back inevitably to the opponent himself. He has thus attained a state of absolute non-resistance.

"Nature is broad and profound. The more you advance, the more you see ahead of you. Aikido is a way without end, harmonious with Nature."

"I am just in the first grade in Aikido and I am still practicing it. I will continue to do so all the rest of my life and leave Aikido as an inheritance for the generations to come."

Thus Professor Uyeshiba expresses his belief humbly and quietly and puts his belief into practice as he preaches.

Admirals such as Isamu Takeshita, Sankichi Takahashi, Hidesuke Yamamoto, and other flag officers received instruction from him Men of noble families such as Sameshima and Matsudaira were also among his students.

These students undoubtedly admired his unrivaled mastery of the arts, but they were even more attracted to his mentality and distinguished personality.

When World War II began, Professor Uyeshiba for reasons of his own left the *Dojo,* built a hut in the mountains of Ibaragi Prefecture and engaged in farming. After that, for twelve years he devoted himself to mental training.

During this period he did not accept any new pupils, but he brought up a few of the students who were deeply attached to him and went to his mountain hut.

I am one of the fortunate few who are privileged to have close communion with the Professor's personality and receive the mental discipline of Aikido.

For some time after the War, Professor Uyeshiba remained in the mountains and devoted himself leisurely to his training. He saw that post-war morality was at a low ebb among the people and many young men went astray, and he deeply grieved at this tendency. Many self-conceited Japanese who had thought themselves spiritually superior lost self-confidence after the miserable defeat of their nation and even denied the existence of any spirit.

Professor Uyeshiba was convinced that this was the time to reveal Aikido to the public, let them know the proper use of mind and body, let them understand the principles of Nature and let them once more gain back their confidence. He called his former students together and began the spread of Aikido.

Today in Japan many young men and even old men devote themselves day and night to Aikido training. Aikido is also studied in America, France, India and Burma, and many come from all over the world to the headquarters *Dojo* in Tokyo and ask for instruction from Professor Uyeshiba.

The headquarters *Dojo,* located at No. 102, Wakamatsu-cho, Shinjuku-ku, Tokyo, Japan, is currently operated by the Professor's son, Kisshomaru Uyeshiba, of the eighth rank in Aikido.

Professor Uyeshiba appears sometimes at this *Dojo* and himself instructs the young men.

I received permission from Professor Uyeshiba to spread Aikido in America. First I went to Hawaii, started Aikido instruction, and organized Hawaii Aiki Kwai. Over 2000 men practice Aikido and there are over 100 *Yudansha* (black belt holders), and Aikido is being spread to the mainland United States.

In France, there is an instructor, who has attained the sixth rank in Aikido. He has given Aikido instruction for the past six years and is continuing to train many students. Some of them went especially to Japan, remained at the headquarters *Dojo* for a year practicing Aikido.

The spirit of universal love and the rationale of non-resistance are being understood by people all over the world today. It can be said that Professor Uyeshiba's long-cherished desire to contribute even a little to world peace has been fulfilled.

In 1960, he was awarded the Medal of Honor with Purple Ribbon* by the Japanese Government. The following year, he went to Hawaii on the occasion of the completion of Hawaii Aiki Kwai's new *dojo*, and gave exhibitions of his art to the general public and an opportunity to practitioners of Aikido to see the Master at work.

* An honor awarded to those who have made outstanding contributions toward the furtherance of learning, arts, invention, creative work, etc.

6

about the author

Do not criticize any of the other martial arts. Speak ill of others and it will surely come back to you. The mountain does not laugh at the river because it is lowly, nor does the river speak ill of the mountain because it cannot move about.

about the AUTHOR

The author was born in January 1920 in Tokyo, Japan. He was very weak and sickly as a child and was always under a doctor's care. By nature, he was very timid.

At the age of 12 he began to study *Judo* and gradually became quite healthy. He entered the preparatory school of Keio University at age 16 and continued to practice *Judo*. He contracted pleurisy by being hit in the chest and from over-exertion and withdrew from classes for a year.

His year of life in bed was to affect his whole life. Immature though his thoughts were, he began to wonder about human existence and about the chief end of life. Though he did not get any conclusive answers, he realized that in any event he would have to study and train his spirit and his body.

After he returned to school, he was not satisfied with his previous routine of merely listening to lectures so he read any book of cultural value that he could lay his hands on.

He discovered however that though he could acquire knowledge by reading, it did not stay long with him, and though his knowledge advanced, if he did not put that knowledge to practical use, his anguish of mind would increase.

Then the understanding came to him that to master any subject, he must not only read about it but put what he learned into practice.

He began the study of *Zen* and Breathing practice, giving his whole heart and body to mastering them, and did not hesitate to practice any form of asceticism no matter how difficult it might be. When he suffered from pleurisy, his doctor told him not to indulge in severe physical exercise for the rest of his life. Now as he earnestly practiced *Zen* and Breathing, he had no time to worry about his health. While he continued to practice, his health improved until it was perfect. After two years, the doctor could find no trace of the pleurisy even under X-ray.

He practiced thought concentration on his lower abdomen by *Zen* and Breathing, but it was a very difficult art. While he was seated, the art was easy enough, but when he was exercising, concentration was disturbed.

He went back to his *Judo* practice. He was able to concentrate on his lower abdomen at the beginning of practice sessions and he was in fine fettle, but if he was shaken up by contact with a bigger man, his concentration vanished. Though he was able to concentrate his thoughts in the beginning, he could not beat a bigger, stronger man, so he could not be satisfied with *Judo.*

One day he heard about Aikido and Professor Morihei Uyeshiba from a senior Judoist, and called on him with the senior's letter of introduction.

Professor Uyeshiba readily gave him a demonstration and showed him some of the arts with his students. Every movement was so smooth that it looked like a Japanese *Odori* (dance). Whenever several big young men attacked him, they were sent flying.

As the author had practiced *Judo* and struggled with only one man at a time, he could not believe that Professor Uyeshiba's arts were genuine and thought that the whole thing was a frame-up.

After the demonstration, Professor Uyeshiba told the author, "Come and attack me at your pleasure." The author took his coat off and rushed at him with all his strength. He remembered attacking him, but the next moment, he found himself lying on the mat and could not remember how he was thrown or what parts of his body the Professor had touched.

The author had confidence in *Judo* at the time because he could throw any fourth rank black belt Judoist at Keio University, but he was absolutely impotent against Professor Uyeshiba. If he could understand what part of his body received power, he might devise a method of standing up against Professor Uyeshiba, but since he could not understand that, he was powerless against him.

He was glad to find at last the way he had been seeking. He

asked Professor Uyeshiba for permission to become his student. At that time, it was very difficult to become his student, but fortunately for him, he was allowed to do so.

After that, the author practiced Aikido with his whole heart and mind, still continuing to practice *Zen* and Breathing, and he finally mastered the art of concentrating his thought on his lower abdomen.

In Aikido, unless one learns this art, one can be thrown very easily. Concentration on the lower abdomen then is the primary art. Since all Aikido arts are based on reason, the author could practice them and simultaneously continue the feeling of *Zen* of sitting calmly in the mountains, and he could master many matters one by one that he had understood only in his thinking.

During the Second World War, he was in the army for four years, for a while being in the front lines while the War was being waged deep in China, and while under a hail of bullets, he trained himself in *Ki*, mastering it well so that his mind would not wander even under such conditions.

The War ended, he returned to his home and called on his teacher again, and studied many matters which he mastered under war conditions in the practice of Aikido. and he understood the basic principles of the use of *Ki*.

In 1952, when the author was thirty-two years of age, Professor Uyeshiba gave him the eighth rank in Aikido.

In 1953–1954, he introduced Aikido to Hawaii and remained for a year to teach, and in 1955–1956 he taught for another year.

In four years' time he was promoted to the ninth rank, the highest rank in Aikido. In 1961, he went to Hawaii accompanying Professor Uyeshiba on Hawaii Aiki Kwai's invitation to take part in the celebration of the completion of Hawaii Aiki Kwaikan. His engagement in the tropical Islands kept him for well over a year. During that time, he extended his travel to California. At various places in the Pacific Coast States, he taught at many arenas, and returned to Japan in March, 1962. The author plans to make his fifth trip overseas in 1964 in response to the many invitations he has received. He plans to go as far as New York and other points, using California as his home base.

The author wrote this book while he was in Hawaii the fourth time 1961–1962. He is at present the chief instructor at the headquarters of Aikido in Tokyo, Japan.

Glossary

AIKIDO strives truly to understand Nature, to be grateful for her wonderful gifts to us, to make her heart its heart, and to become one with her. This striving for understanding and the practical application of the laws of Nature, expressed in the words Ai and Ki, form the fundamental concept of the art of AIKIDO.

A. Ki

The word most frequently used in Aikido is *Ki*. *Ki* is a very convenient word because it has both a deep meaning connected with nature and a light meaning which is used in daily life. It is very difficult to define *Ki* and even more difficult to translate it into English. Therefore, the word *Ki* will be used in the explanation of Aikido.

In oriental thought, it is said that in the beginning there was chaos. The dust of chaos settled gradually to form the sun, the earth, the moon and the stars. On the earth, the elements combined to become minerals. animal and vegetable life. We call the chaotic condition before the universe took shape *Ki*. We say therefore that all things came from *Ki*.

Ki itself has neither beginning nor end, nor increase nor decrease. Though its shape was changed, *Ki* itself was never changed. We can see many things around us, all made from *Ki*, and when they lose their shape, their elements return to *Ki*. Depending on what you believe, you call it God, or Buddha or Akua or some other name.

Aikido is the way of at-one-ment with cosmic power or *Ki*.

That is the deep meaning of *Ki*.

What is the light meaning of *Ki* used in our daily life? A good feeling, a bad feeling, a great feeling, timidity, vigor, courage, a retiring disposition, et cetera—these are terms used in our daily life. In each word or phrase, the Japanese use *Ki* as an integral part. The reason is that a human being was created from *Ki* of the universe. While he receives *Ki*, he is alive. Deprive him of *Ki* and he dies; he loses his human shape. So long as his body is filled with *Ki* and it pours forth abundantly, he is vigorous and filled with courage. On the contrary, when his body has run out of *Ki*, he is weak, cowardly and retiring.

In Aikido training, we make every effort to learn to fill our body with *Ki* and use it powerfully. Therefore, we must understand well the deep meaning of *Ki*.

(1) Ki Wo Neru—To train your *Ki*

The meaning of training your *Ki* is that you believe that your body is filled with *Ki* of the universe so you keep the one point, make it the center of your body and pour forth *Ki* from your whole body. You must train it in every movement of the Aikido arts.

(2) Ki Wo Totonoeru—To prepare your *Ki*

You keep your mind at the one point, let your breathing be calm and keep yourself calm, ready to move quickly at any time.

(3) Ki Wo Dasu—To pour forth *Ki*

Like an unbendable arm, if you think that your power is gushing out through your arm, it become very strong and difficult to bend. Such use of the mind is called pouring forth *Ki*.

If you believe that your *Ki* is gushing forth, your *Ki* is really gushing out. For example, as you are walking along and someone pushes you by your shoulder. If you pull your *Ki* inward or your mind trails behind your body, your attacker will be able to push you back or throw you down. If you pour forth your *Ki* and your mind is ahead of your body, he will not be able to push you back, but instead he himself will be pushed back by the impact.

Let us say there is clear water gushing out from a spring in a muddy stream. As long as this water gushes out, muddy water cannot get into the spring. But if the clear water stops flowing for even a moment, muddy water will enter the spring immediately.

Ki is like this spring water. As long as your *Ki* is being poured forth, your opponent's *Ki* does not come upon you. Stop pouring forth your *Ki* or pull your *Ki* inward and your opponent's power will engage you instantly.

If you would gain true understanding, you must practice diligently the art of pouring forth a constant stream of *Ki*. Master this and you will be able to see whether or not your opponent pours out his *Ki* merely by looking at his form and posture.

The power which is not directed against you is nothing for you to worry about, though it may be very strong. If you would understand non-resistance or non-aggression, the essential principle of Aikido, you must first practice pouring forth your *Ki*.

The reasoning back of non-resistance is not to run away from your opponent's strength but so to maneuver that his *Ki* does not engage you; make him lose his aggressive urge. This is the real victory. You may fell your opponent but as long as you leave him with the urge to attack, there may come a day when you will be defeated by him. The real victory comes when you expunge from his mind this urge to attack.

(4) Ki No Nagare—The stream of *Ki*

Whenever you keep pouring forth your *Ki* and swinging your arms, you draw a circle or a line that resembles a continuous stream of water. Such a stream is called "the stream of *Ki*."

If you set a point on the ground and use a length or rope as your radius, you can make a circle. Of course, the rope must be held taut or the circle will not be perfect. If you continuously pour forth your *Ki* and keep the one point, your hands will naturally move in a circle. If your *Ki* is poured forth sporadically, your form becomes ragged and you lose power. Then you move your body, as you move your one point too, your hands make eccentric circles and revolutions. Like illustrations, a, b, and c, your stream can take many shapes and you can whirl your opponent into the strong stream of your *Ki* and throw him.

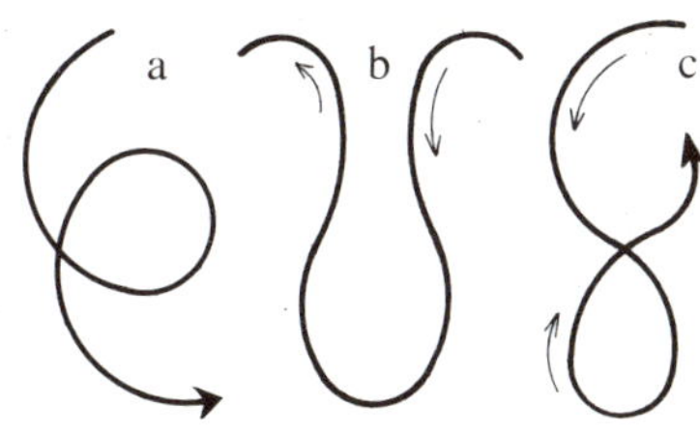

(5) Ki Wo Kiru—To cut *Ki*

To cut *Ki* means to cut the stream of *Ki*. If your mind becomes frozen or you pull your *Ki* inward for even a moment, your stream of *Ki* is cut off and its power will likewise be cut off.

As an analogy, once you start pushing a cart, momentum keeps it going with not too much effort on your part. If you stop, you must fight inertia to get it moving again.

If you continue the stream of *Ki* and do not cut it, you can lead your opponent by bringing him into your stream of *Ki* and letting his power go back against himself, so that throwing him down will be quite easy.

When you cut your *Ki* at any time, his *Ki* will come upon you immediately and you will not be able to move him. You must practice always not to cut your *Ki* but to continue to pour it forth.

(6) Ki Ga Nukeru—To lose *Ki*

To lose *Ki* means that you have forgotten your one point and are in no condition to pour forth your *Ki*. When you are disappointed or discouraged or tired of your work, put the cause down as loss of *Ki*.

You will never succeed in anything if you lose your *Ki*. Especially since Aikido is the training of *Ki*, it is better to stop practicing if you are doing it without *Ki* because that will cause you to form bad habits. You must always put your *Ki* into your training.

B. Kokyu

The words *Kokyu Ho* and *Kokyu Nage* are used very often in Aikido. There are many kinds of arts especially in *Kokyu Nage*, with numerous movements and variations of these for each *Kokyu Nage* art.

Kokyu is, in plain words, the movement of your *Ki* or the movement of your body following *Ki.*

If you have strong *Kokyu,* your body is filled with powerful *Ki* and you are moving and throwing your opponent correctly. In other forms of *Budo,* or the martial arts, the phrase "strong power" is used, but in Aikido, we say strong *Kokyu* because the arts of Aikido are concerned not only with physical matters but also with *Ki.* *Kokyu Ho* is the way that leads others by *Kokyu,* and *Kokyu Nage* is the art of throwing others by *Kokyu.*

C. Hanmi

Always face your opponent in the posture of *Hanmi.* If you stand before him, keeping your feet together, your mind will be fixed there and you will have difficulty in moving when he attacks you. To stand with your left foot a half step forward is called Left *Hammi* and with your right foot a half step forward, Right *Hanmi.*

The stance keeps you strong in the rear yet you can move swiftly at will by using both feet, each one acting in concert with the other. With this stance you do not put the center of gravity of your body on one leg only but on your one point and you must stand as though by mind and not by your legs, so that you can defend yourself against any attack by your opponent.

D. Ma - Ai

In a real fight, the distance between you and your opponent is important. If you approach too close, you cannot maneuver in avoiding a sudden attack. If on the other hand you keep yourself too far from him, it will be difficult for you to use the arts against him. You must keep a proper distance, not too close nor too far away from him. To keep the proper distance between you and your opponent is called taking *Ma-ai.*

If you always pour forth your *Ki,* you will understand naturally how to take *Ma-ai* according to the height of your body. If you pull your *Ki* inward, you will lose the *Ma-ai.* It is by forgetting to take *Ma-ai* that some one will stick his neck out, so to speak, and get his block knocked off.

The distance from which your opponent must take one step forward to attack you and from which you must take one step forward to attack him is generally considered good *Ma-ai.*

When you are closer than this *Ma-ai,* you must already be holding him down.

E. *Orenai Te*—Unbendable arm

It is called Unbendable Arm when you pour forth your *Ki* through it and it is difficult to bend even though you do not put any strength into it.

Nobody can put strength into his arm constantly. If you are strong only while you put forth strength, it will be useless when something suddenly happens about you.

Be relaxed at all times and still strong at any time you choose. Unbendable Arm does not depend on the angle of the arm. If you continue to pour out your *Ki*, your arm is always unbendable.

F. *Fudo No Shisei*—Immovable posture

Immovable posture does not mean one from which you cannot move easily but one in which you keep your mind on the one point, relax the rest of your body and fill it with *Ki*. It means the posture in which your mind is not disturbed by anything; neither is your body moved. When you do move, your mind and body must move in coordination.

G. *Irimi*

When your opponent's power is coming toward you and yours against his, there will be a head-on collision and the stronger will win. *Irimi* is the way to advance toward your opponent, not meeting him with resistance but leading his power at will. To understand *Irimi*, you must keep your one point and Unbendable Arm or you cannot make *Irimi* work for you. *Irimi* is the special art found only in Aikido.

It enables you to demonstrate directly the principle of the art of non-resistance, letting your opponent's power return to himself no matter how powerful he may be.

H. *Tenkan*

Tenkan is the way to lead your opponent's power without stopping it, by turning your body when his power is coming toward you. In *Irimi*, you must sometimes move in a strong, straight line, but in *Tenkan*, you must always move in a strong circular movement or revolution. You can suck in an opponent's power into your *Tenkan* movement and let his power dissipate itself so that you can subsequently lead him to fall down.

Almost all of the Aikido arts are used on both *Irimi* and *Tenkan*.

I. Nage

Nage is the one who is attacked by his opponent and throws him down.

J Uke

Uke is the one who attacks the other and is thrown by him.